Delicate Bait

Akron Series in Poetry

Also by Roger Mitchell

POETRY

Savage Baggage
Braid
The Word For Everything
Adirondack
A Clear Space on a Cold Day
Moving
Letters from Siberia and Other Poems

NONFICTION

Clear Pond: The Reconstruction of a Life

Akron Series in Poetry

Elton Glaser, Editor

Barry Seiler, *The Waters of Forgetting*
Raeburn Miller, *The Comma After Love: Selected Poems of Raeburn Miller*
William Greenway, *How the Dead Bury the Dead*
Jon Davis, *Scrimmage of Appetite*
Anita Feng, *Internal Strategies*
Susan Yuzna, *Her Slender Dress*
Raeburn Miller, *The Collected Poems of Raeburn Miller*
Clare Rossini, *Winter Morning with Crow*
Barry Seiler, *Black Leaf*
William Greenway, *Simmer Dim*
Jeanne E. Clark, *Ohio Blue Tips*
Beckian Fritz Goldberg, *Never Be the Horse*
Marlys West, *Notes for a Late-Blooming Martyr*
Dennis Hinrichsen, *Detail from* The Garden of Earthly Delights
Susan Yuzna, *Pale Bird, Spouting Fire*
John Minczeski, *Circle Routes*
Barry Seiler, *Frozen Falls*
Melody Lacina, *Private Hunger*
George Bilgere, *The Good Kiss*
William Greenway, *Ascending Order*
Roger Mitchell, *Delicate Bait*
Lynn Powell, *The Zones of Paradise*

Delicate Bait

Poems by

Roger Mitchell

The University of Akron Press
Akron, Ohio

 First Edition 2003.
07 06 05 04 03 5 4 3 2 1

All inquiries and permissions requests should be addressed to the publisher,
The University of Akron Press, Akron, OH 44325–1703

LIBRARY OF CONGRESS CATALOGING-IN-PUBLICATION DATA
Mitchell, Roger, 1935-
Delicate bait : poems / by Roger Mitchell.– 1st ed.
p. cm. — (Akron series in poetry)
ISBN 1-931968-06-3 (cloth: alk. paper) – ISBN 1-931968-07-1 (pbk. : alk. paper)
I. Title. II. Series.
PS3563.I82D45 2003
811'.54–DC22
2003019704

Manufactured in the United States of America.
The paper used in this publication meets the minimum requirements of American National Standard for Information Sciences—Permanence of Paper for Printed Library Materials, ANSI Z39.48–1984. ∞

Cover: *Still Life with Fish and Leeks,* Ng Eng Teng. Courtesy of NUS Museums, National University of Singapore.

For Dorian, again

Contents

I

II

I

Aunt El

She was said to have never bathed.
And to have stacked the rooms
of her house with newspapers.
I don't even know whose aunt she was.
Maybe nobody's aunt. Aunt Blank.
Though the glee in mother's eyes,
as she hands me the keys to this
damp closet, tells me, of course, what else.

I see her rattling about with a wagon
or bag, draped in a straggling dress
and bonnet, asking at back doors, cringing
under the stares of housegirls and cooks.
She couldn't have done it alone,
on her subscription, presuming she had one.
Presuming, too, she could read.
Maybe she needed to fill a room
in a hurry, to admire her handiwork,
to say, this is my room full of words.
She would say this to no one, of course,
thinking that no one would ever know.
There she is in a robe, tattered. She holds
the lantern away from her body,
as though she were paper herself.

There were farms somewhere
in back of my family, a barn
in back of my grandparents' house.
The people who live there now know nothing
about us, don't see the spot of blood
on the driveway, the ambulance idling

at the side door, don't see Aunt El
or her baffled eyes, going her rounds
in a stinking skirt, talking to dogs,
scattering children like flies. Even
the chickens avoided her mournful cluck.

Nor do they see the mayor of Avalon,
or the priest who lived with his sister,
the unmarried schoolteacher, the man
who ran out on his wife, or the one
who stole. They don't see the man
who killed himself drinking or the woman,
his wife, he left with the children,
or the chauffeured limousine with someone,
concealed, in back. And certainly
they don't see Bertha, dead on the floor
of her unheated house in Camden.

I come from somewhere I've never been,
or somewhere I've been but don't remember.
I need to know that I've been where I've been
and lived there and loved what there was to love.
If I could, I would choose this woman, this aunt
whom no one mentioned (and no one forgot),
to take me there. She teaches me how to knock
at a back door, how to ask the smallest question.

Outside of Town

The name was Canaday, a doctor, friend
of my father's. He lived outside of town.
A doctor with a farm. I don't know why
I spent the night there. Before dinner, though,
or was it breakfast, I was asked, at least
I think I was, if I wanted to watch
the cook, her husband, somebody, wring
a chicken's neck. It walked around the yard
for several minutes. Looking for its head,
I thought. The doctor must have worked in town.
It was our town, too. My uncle used to drive
me out to Clayt's for buttermilk. He loved
something about the name, Clayt, cows, the barn.
And getting something straight from the source.

Destin

'44, the last summer of the war
for Dad, four months in a fishing village
on the Gulf, rotted wharf, one-room schoolhouse.
I don't think I wore shoes the whole time.
We knew our neighbors, little else,
while Dad commuted to the base. Mom
baked pies, it seemed, each day. Mornings swimming
in the Chocktahawtchee with the rays, sting rays,
sunsets on Silver Beach. You could look
to each horizon and see sand only,
where now the condos elbow in to feed.
Which is why, I suppose, it was here
a crazed pilot, on leave from bombing Europe
into rubble, banked and came about one day,
and catching us alone in paradise,
buzzed us into crabs scurrying for a hole.
I ran, but I looked up at the bright blur
of wing and fuselage. I may have waved.
That could have been the week of D-day,
though I was nine and have no memory
of what I've now seen fifty times in reruns.

Reading the Latest History of the Bomb

I never saw such white suits, streets that thought
could cross with its eyes closed. Nor ever read
such knocked-together prose. Here is a past no one
wanted, one they pulled apart, forgot,
or highwayed into sunning by the pool.
The paint has faded and the struts rotted
away, and yet, like a bad patch, a poorly
mended bone, the purposes are plain.

"All those kids," Truman brought himself to say
the day after Nagasaki. He said it
to his Cabinet. In closed session.
Fifty-two years later, it reached me.
Though I was there. And heard the news. And,
like everybody else, I'm sure, cheered.

Spinout

We spend more of our lives on the phone these days,
wondering back and forth across the continent what

each other is doing and whether it will ever happen again,
that we will all be in the same room saying, again,

"I don't know how she does it" or "wouldn't it be great if."
Some of us are gone, of course, and others are moving on,

though not that deliberately and not, as you might guess,
with the high tight grip we threw into that drive

across country in the fifties, the one that took three days
and ended in a bunkhouse behind a bowling alley in Aspen.

All that frozen corn stubble for a few dozen slashes
down a mountainside so fast you thought your skin was flame,

ten pins banging in your dreams and the shouted snow
spangling the sun and the yips coming up your throat pipe

as the mountain disappeared beneath you and you
almost wanted to, as well, as long as it was glass and shattered.

Well, who knows. You went back, all the way back.
Three days and two nights in a two-door Chevy, slush

in Kansas, rain across the Mississippi, places you had
never seen, coffee shops and diners, a spinout in Missouri

where you might have died, but didn't, were lucky, again,
as you always were, dread and ecstasy vying for the right

to eat your bones, your jackrabbit happiness, and winning,
both of them. In the photos, grinning, with a wrinkled brow.

The Next One

I forget his name, but all one summer
I was his charge. He must have hated that.
A college kid with no more brains than to
marvel how he could shovel all day long,
try to imitate, with no aptitude
or skill, fall into bed at night cursing,
and then forget. I can still see him thrust,
pause, tilt, and throw. He showed up sharp at six
each morning, grim in his bib overalls,
his readiness to work without a break,
a word, a thought for anything but thrust,
pause, tilt, and throw, till he came to some end,
promised but withheld, end he could not name,
or would not tell the boy who, he was sure,
would go back home at the end of summer,
only a visitor to the world he knew.
He showed me how to throw an irrigation pipe.
You hold your hand over the near end
and toss it across the dike. Water flows
into the row. Then you do the next one.

Listening

I can still hear Robert Frost. He was the first.
Who struggled up to the front, his white hair tossed
across his eyes. The undergraduates grinned
to hear a man snap twigs among the scholars.
I remember Auden, too, in the great hall
at Balliol, telling us he was sick.
He had come home to die, and he was sick,
he said, of "the whole fucking lot" of us.
He read for an hour without books or notes.
I can't remember what he read that night,
November in Chicago, but Lowell bowed
and thanked us at the end, a man half dragged
ashore, a fish thrashed out of water.
Basil Bunting, in London, reading *Briggflatts*
in his chopped Northumbrian brogue.
Kinnell stood up in Milwaukee once
and said, before his own, the hard poem
called "Hard Rock" by the poet Etheridge Knight.
And here in Bloomington, Hugo, holding
the crab at bay. In two months, he had lost
a lung. In two years, died. He, too, recited,
hands palms down on the stone slab in front of him.
And Olson. I sat in the chapel pew
at Beloit, the songs across my lap,
and watched his poems jackknife across the page.
John Berryman in Madison, jerking
his Henry on a stick, Merrill whispering
into his book, the look of a thinking
monkey on his face. Vohznesensky
nailed his Russian poems to the floor.
Ginsberg with finger cymbals, Rothenberg

with gourds. Duncan conducted, unfolding poems
in the air, birds of a single wing.
Leather-jacketed Ted Hughes, resonant
and stolid, stood with one hand hidden.
Empson at Oxford, a squeaking reed.
MacDiarmid in full main at Edinburgh.
Kizer in Manchester. The pale MacNeice.
And Kunitz at the embassy in Warsaw.
Where, to six or seven, he read his poem
on having his pocket picked in Rome. But more,
he read the one I read his whole work twice to find.

In Paterson I tried to buy that poem
in a store. They thought it was a joke.
I read Venetian history for a year,
only to have Pound die before I got there.
I had our conversations all worked out.
He would read me the thirteenth canto,
and I would come back with that song from Lawes.
He would say something, then, I don't know what,
and the long slide of history would stop
long enough to blur before our consciousness.
We would see it, though, a swipe across the sky,
and say, "There it is" or "There it is, there,"
before the call to dinner or the nurse
with medicines took everything away.

I don't know what I thought that day, if it was
a day, and not a year or mere flash of sunlight
off the gray river in the afternoon

or taint of bookdust at the Grolier,
but I remember hearing words I knew,
or thought I knew, handled like rough stone,
sharpened like a stick.

I read a poem in a book then, too,
put it down, forgot it, went on living.
And somewhere, later, when I wasn't looking,
the light changed suddenly or the thing
I thought I was got up and walked away.

Go Ahead

Go ahead, said the great crested flycatcher,
lie in your bed all morning with the yellow curtains drawn
and write poetry. No one will see.

Strange Bloom

There's a car parked at the side of the house
so deep in weeds you'd think they'd found a way
to bring the twentieth century back
from its errand to the moon. Strange bent blossoms
of rust and chrome dangle off the stalk
of summer. The gas pump by the walk
says nineteen cents. A gallon of that air
would go a nickel in Niagara Falls.
And yes, you can go back to griddlecakes.
The griddle's in the grass there. A hog pen
full of strangled mud swoops backward to a field
where forty kinds of weed play keepaway.
Who was it draped the snake across the doorknob?
Who was it made that feral bloom
of smashed glass in the fireplace,
flame of damnation and indifference?
The dentist in town, twenty miles away,
who bought the whole idea of the past,
says when you ask him, even kindly, no.
Not to you, but to something that your voice
over the phone at night brings back to him.
Moonlight over the unpainted clapboard fence
and a life he knew he'd one day have to buy
and drop there, rotting, where he found it.
You say you understand, and maybe you do.

At the Mall, Late

An arrangement
of twelve towels
in dark light,
a few drifting
customers, us,
late at night.
Nobody wants
anything now.
Even the young
shopgirl yawns,
dreams she is leaning
on the clean glass
she leans on.
This is the hour
we've come to, late,
want hushed in us,
the world
made visible
and still. To be
among bright
plentiful things,
to stand among
tanned mannequins.
Outside, a few
stray cars in the lot,
light on a high pole,
wet asphalt.

To Molly on Her Sixteenth Birthday

This memory, sharp as the day it came,
of you at the school yard gate. Of the light
as we passed through the silent streets of Oadby,
the houses crisp, the lawns immaculate
and small. Of my saying, though not out loud, this
is the morning, and this, again, is the start
of something. What, I could not yet know.

And there, at the gate, it was, where you stopped
and, turning, said, as gently as you could,
"I want to go by myself now." This glimpse,
you gliding swiftly up the empty walk,
alert, eleven, a little afraid,
but going forward, I give you to keep.

Truth of the Matter

for Bridget

I remember the dreamy deer in the park at Oxford
grazing under the evenly cropped trees.
The leaves came down from the sky and stopped
just above the heads of the placid deer,
who, when they cared, poured like muscled water
through the trunks, appearing and disappearing
among them, herding together, their stick little legs
breaking the silence barely among the leaves
which all came down in a line like a shade.

The day I came to watch from behind the fence
the innocent gray deer prink in their perfect park,
away from the traffic on High Street, away, too,
from the great names of the dead, the ghosts
of the living, agog, moving among them, touching
the stones, saying the strange names aloud
in a twisted tongue, phrases mastered at breakfast,
standing, rapt, where the martyr stood alone
or running a finger down the spine of a book.

On that day, tired of the fixed stare of the great
greatness, from which we had only partly come,
from which we had barely come at all, in fact,
watching the frail deer, posing themselves beneath the oaks,
which all came down like thick lava and stopped,
stuck in the air, I knew when the dog had come.

I did not see it at first, and was not sure
what it was, when the men ran panting past,
waving their arms, and the deer flashed in
and out of the shadows, sinewy and pert, turning
and leaping in unison, a real corps de ballet.

One of them died that day, and the dog was caught
and, somewhere out of the way, killed.
I remember it loping out of the woods,
slavering its bloody jaws, cornered at last.
It stood while the wheezing men undid its collar.
And my youngest daughter, three at the time,
who understood nothing, from whom I tried,
wrongly perhaps, to keep the truth of the matter, cried.

There We Are

I've had my beard now half my life. It's mine,
this face. It's half a lifetime since I showed
up hairy at my brother's wedding. He
got thrown in a pool, drink and all. I got looks.
That was the summer English had the stuff,
and we beat Dairy Science for the crown.
The summer Gordon Thompson said those words
I'd never heard—"Have a nice life"—and went
away and had one, so I hear. He
played second base. That was the summer, too,
we camped one night on Lake Cayuga, up
at the north end. It was the end of summer.
We had seen my brother wed, and dried,
and were headed home. The sky was clear,
a golden rose. The air at dusk had bite.
We were just putting things away. The bed,
a few rough planks laid side by side across
the engine housing, a van we later drove
to Denver in a blizzard. Sally shouted.
Across the entire sky, a line of huge
slow birds, whether cranes or swans I didn't know
enough to tell then, pushing calmly on.

I think of all the uses memory
is put to, bandages and wine. This one

I'd like to leave there, with Gordon smiling
wryly at his wit, English by some
miracle victorious, my brother
going joyful through the door, Sally
shouting at the sky, oh look, and me
about to show my brand new face to mother.
There we are, all of us, pushing calmly on.

Venice, 1979

The vaporetto rocked the chocolate water.
A man approached and, in a cautious tone,
spoke my name. You, it is you, is it not?
It was. And later in a cramped taverna,
the salty carcasses of small-boned fish,
an hour of reminiscing, watered wine.
Someone was singing, I remember, another
being sick. She was with me then, and he,
whom I had known in another life, had only
a little of his boyishness turned back
at the edges. For both, I had to translate.
What I was shook hands with what I had been.
They were on friendly terms, though distant.
She and I would marry for a time.
Him, I would never see again. Europe
would collapse, Venice sink another inch.
It seemed important once to go there. Culture,
after all, our dark beginnings. Now,
I mow the lawn another time. Winter
is coming. Winter, that I have always loved.

Repairman

I asked him guardedly where he lived—
on what street, to be exact—before
telling him I knew the place, told him
I had lived in the same town years before.
Why I bothered mentioning it, I don't know.
I lived a few short years there, years at the time
I would have traded almost anything—
not that I had much—to get away from.
He was on his knees in gray work pants,
tightening a bolt, before I noticed
the light gray epaulettes painted along
the shoulders of his matching shirt, as though
he were a private in an army of gray
soldiers who fight things that come apart
and had lives the rest of us left behind.
He was glad to be going home at the end of day
(I told him I could see it in my mind)
and spoke ardently of getting up at night
and driving through a snowstorm to aid
people peering out of darkened windows,
wrapped in blankets, not sure if anyone
would come or, come spring, where they'd find themselves.
His boots were scuffed into soft stones.
His hands likewise were roughened leather.
And his name was Bruce, as the tag across
his chest proclaimed in light gray bas-relief.
The man who took a life I might have lived
and lived it came to the house today and told me
not to worry. Nothing broke he couldn't fix.

Motels

This would do as well as any abandoned cottage
on a cliff above the sea, the long grass waving
in what would have been a pasture or sown field.
This might have been a pasture, too, at one time,
with sheep grazing at the foot of the bed
and the farmer, swaddled in revery,
slouching across the road from the Burger King.
He cannot imagine anything like this
happening to the world.

I could do this among coffee shops, too,
bookstores, restaurants, ballet and the theatre.
A certain table or booth,
a checked tablecloth with stains,
long philosophical conversations
followed by long silent walks alone
or speeches to the stars.

It is not easy to create such pure transience.
It is true that the Burger King is just across the road,
and that the road is constant with traffic,
and that the whole of Albany
is a few miles to the southeast.
These things do not reduce remoteness, as we know,
but make a landscape in which it can occur,
a place where the wind, in fact, has an exact fit.
I can go to the front desk
and ask the night clerk for a bar of soap,

and without looking at me
or at the soap, he can place it in my hand.
I can shower. And, when I am through,
shower again. And all that time
the television is on.
It is not necessary to watch television
for there to be television,
as it is not necessary for me to look in the mirror
for there to be mirrors everywhere.

The person who slept here last night
left nothing behind, no hair in the sink,
no fingerprint on the glass. He got away
and is eating now at the Burger King across the road
from his new motel. Or taking a shower
with the television on, or looking for something
in the mirror. I judge from the bed
he must have been large, or the person before him,
or all the people who have thrown themselves down
here on this bed in this place, night after night.

Through the wall, a man coughs once.
In an hour, he coughs again. Again, once.
Each time it is a flat, hard hack.
From somewhere else, an hour of machine gun fire,
explosions, groans, shrieks.
And somewhere above me, or below,
the low tones under the muffled words,
the hum on which the words float,
of two people talking urgently through the night.

Taxi Dancer, Montana, 1936

from a photo by Margaret Bourke-White

A grin and a two dollar bill
go a long ways in Montana.
No, I don't know his name,
though he says it's Earl. I say,
fine. The other one's Buck.
Do you like my new shoes?
I went to a store in Missoula,
high ceilings and all.
I like being pretty, and someday
I'm going to be happy. Earl
has his hand where it ought not
be, but he'd take it away
if I asked. Go ahead, look.
It don't cost a penny to dream.
Someday I'm going to be ugly.
I'm going to be sad, too,
sadder than flower print dresses,
scuffed boards on a floor.
But not now, not tonight.

Museum of Local History

Amos Throop, citizen of this small
stretch of the glacial underscarp,
I see you scraping through the flattened
underbrush along some creek,
doing your humble "pish" to flush
the catbird from its nest. And there,
cigar-box ornithologist,
you place the smooth, blue-gray shells
in their exact compartment, room
of odd nostalgias, banjos, teeth,
dust-throttled pelt. In the next room,
a thing someone slithered off
the body of a soldier, son
of the rising sun, a hand-sewn swath
of white cotton, folded inward,
sewn shut, with prayers for his return.
In the new and newly vandalized
public library, an old man
stumbles up the words headfirst.
I think he wants to read, Amos.
I think he took the river road
down past the dam one time and came
back shamed. I think he looked at all
that corn again and cried. His sons,
what were they, and those stumps thrown
around the yard, the woodchuck in
a heap beside the road. Amos,
I'm sorry, but they've closed forever
Miller's Department Store. No more

tuxedos for the senior prom.
The coffee here is river-run,
partly, the other part a shape
clouds make caroming across grass.
I don't know, but the food here
worries me. The way they lift it
to their mouths. They want something
from it that isn't on the label.
Maybe it's fine, but at the edge
of town, a roller coaster dips
like the flight of some flightless bird,
and, though winter is almost done,
it doesn't hide the five stone hammers
in a case someone broke his plow
against. Was that you, Amos, you
pounding down the rows, wondering
what else the limestone might reveal,
what egg the earth might lay, what bird
could fly so far away it stayed?
They had a room, I'm told, for the bones
of their own seeing, a room sewn shut
with pale, late-winter light and dust.
A mother looked behind her once
but didn't see the GI lean
across the sea, untie the ties,
and pull from under the stilled weight
of her son the fiery stitches.
Blunt hammers in a case, winter
breaking up, and mud. The road out
may be the same as the one in,
but you have to face the other way.

Why We're Here

Before we can properly excuse ourselves,
I am sitting in the shade under the oak tree
talking about farming with the old man,
and my wife is out among the flowers
with his wife. I know nothing about farming,
but the words fall effortlessly from my mouth.
My wife comes back holding an iris clipping,
and they join us in the shade with the flies.
We are suddenly members of the family,
rocking and swatting. We talk about things
as though we had waited all winter long
for the snow to melt. A bluebird
flies into the box on the fencepost
as we talk, and a rabbit hops lethargically
across the driveway down by the car
where I left the mower I brought
to be sharpened. That's why we're here.

He is the last man in the county
who can sharpen a push mower.
And he is not easy to find. And
he takes his time. We have found him, though,
and he is taking most of the afternoon
to tell us he thinks he can do it
and for how much. We shake on it.

I am getting my mower sharpened
by first having my flaked faith in the ways of people
touched up and my disinclination to old age
abated. It is costing me eight dollars.

Retirements in the Neighborhood

Jim has that look already, a little
like soup. Not that he ever clutched his beer
that tight, as when he wandered out to talk
to the hydrangeas or hand me his last ten
bean plants to put where I might find dirt.
If I ever stopped granulating the clay, that is,
or twanging the tines on the garden fork,
which I have often thought more spiritual
than hammering, more transcendental
than grass, than waiting till the cabbage moth,
tomato blight, grackle, or slug had borne off
the summer, the sweat, the slowed-down days.
Last night a storm blew in and caught us dead
center. The heat arrived and the long
dripping afternoons, nights pasted to sheets,
to swearing never to do this again, never
to let a thing so unmindful as beets
or a job, a yard full of weeds, a sock,
the pounded, intractable, rabbit-brained
clay of all clays own what we were or take
the sting, the long, sweet sting of beer, away.
For we were not made, but came to be, and glad
we were that the storm tore through us, though
Jim's hand shakes and the tree we thought still with us
snapped. There it is, hollow, dead it seems
for years, in a bed of its own true leaves.

Clearing in the West

for my father, dying

In the midst of being awake on a Tuesday.
Walking the heartless corridor in the heat,
head petrified with memo and deadline.
Pacing the edges of a way of doing things
I once knew the need of, he now responding
with his eyes only. You say something
to him, and he closes them. Or moves them off
in the direction of the innocuous curtain.
What use is speech? What are we doing here,
and why are there these thousand miles?
I read a fistful of poems in a taxi,
and maybe this is the moment, humidity
ninety percent, leaves gasping for breath,
a thankless thin blue to the sky and all
these fresh frightened faces clustered
around the bed asking for their turn. Move over,
they say. I get to carry the pole now.
I get to paddle in back. It's clearing, he'd say,
clearing in the west. And so we rode
on hope and the bad road for another
thousand afternoons. Now the west is here.
The wide awful brim of a tired hat.
May the way be clear, the way west.
May the clouds part and you, the hard blue sky,
bend a little, bend down and take this bag
of hope who loved nothing more than your blueness.
Whether you showed it to him or not.

Thrown Back Light

Not that I couldn't find my way, but more
than sixty years went by before I reached
Walden. The day after, I put my face
against the glass of Melville's Arrowhead.
There was no one home, though I heard footsteps
deep inside the house, a door slam, silence.
The woods I stood in Henry never saw,
though through the window I could just make out
a spoon Melville might have lifted to his mouth.
Worlds wilder than mine, but not as wild
as the yoked life the Shakers led across
the valley, where the barns stand still and the high
square windows of gray glass threw back the light
they had no use for, drained of its raw fire.

On a Chinese Scroll, *Composing Poetry on a Spring Outing* (Late 12TH Century)

In Kansas City for
one day, I have just read
to a group of young writers
at the arts high school.
They were not all dressed
in the same kind of robe,
as these are, nor did they
wander in the wooded
spaces of the hour,
looking for the day's
instructions. No one,
as yet, stares back at them
down centuries of thought,
wondering why this one
sits by herself or that one
looks sideways at her hand.
One of them asked how
I came to be a poet.
I told them what I know,
the worn story of wanting
what I heard once in a clutch
of words, words I knew
but could not understand.
I still don't understand
what good will come to the boy
who came in late in pants
that don't fit and a look

that looks so far across
his life he sees it
happening in a place
they haven't thought of yet.
I like to think that he
will be there in a corner
of some word, some image,
that no one understands,
writing the great poem
of daylight in Kansas
City, Kansas City
Transformation, one day
in the hard life of those
held prisoner by it.
His eyes are closed. He dreams
the centuries are gone,
are going, and the life
he knows, which is mine, too,
is coming to a kind
conclusion there, a clutch
of words crackling with breath.

Letter to Jim Doyle

Dear Jim,
This is maybe the tenth time in a month
that I've flipped open a lit magazine
down at the Book Corner (trying to find,
not what the poets in Ghana are up to—
remember *New World Writing?* Not so new
any more, is it?—but the ones in Rifle,
San Luis Obispo, Martinsville, Bedford),
and bang, there you are. James, of course, not Jim.
Giving the universe the kind of hell
we generally reserve for the neighbor.
I don't know how to get around this snaggle
exactly, the one where you hate the thing
you love, but reading your poems, I lose track.
It's got to have been thirty-five years at least
since I last saw you and not many fewer
since I heard from you, but silence across
a lifetime leaves room, if it's there, for thought.
I remember, and often think about,
the day you walked into my office, fresh
from your own office at the State House and, neither
student nor brother, asked if you could show me
your poems. Having taught now half your life
yourself, you know what a thrill that was,
a poetry walk-on, someone who wrote
because he had to, someone who loved it,
someone who knew it would change his life.
The years in between have been good to me,
as good, I've come to believe, as years can be,

and though I can hear the fluctuations
flitting about in your poems like bats
that find their way into the house, it's clear
you know how to dodge them, or if you can't
dodge the wobble of most things human, look
straight at it and call it a human name.
In the poetry of ancient China
somewhere, one poet is writing another
in a fit of drunken melancholy.
There are at least twenty snowy mountains,
a lifetime, and a blackbird between them.
The poet urges his pen forward, but
the only moving thing is his one thought:
This letter might not reach you, but be well,
and keep writing. The blackbird has begun to smell.

For a Christening in Innishannon

It was every kind of a day that day.
Across the way the cows lay down in the field,
so it rained. And then stood up. So, of course,
it stopped. They had buried a man none of us
knew in the morning, though by afternoon
we had seen the lean of his hurling stick
left at the altar and heard he was good
at the crossword puzzle. They say he died
without warning, though they had the whole
of his life to get ready and a six-foot gash
in the ground besides. The cars lined up
on the grass for mass, and the short-haired boys
lounged by the door. What they were waiting for,
we hadn't a clue, though the sheen shone
on their faces and the day drove slowly by.
Enda Finbarr, in no rush, but ready,
you take your place, a stranger and brother,
in a thing the ages have no name for,
though all of us were there and ate the cake
and looked at the hills that wouldn't hold still,
the clouds dappling our memory
with shadow and light, the next of kin,
the next in line, the mother, the father,
and the wholly unreportable weather.

Milton's Grave

No cranny among official poets
for this one. No stony oratory
for a blind old revolutionary,
about whom I scratched illegible notes
under the buttoned-down gaze of John Major
in the accidents of my awakening
to the random and half-concealed murmurings
in Wyatt and the later Donne in Boulder.
"On or near this spot," says the shallowly
incised stone by the altar. The old woman,
after several tries, threw up her palms
and limped down the aisle (was I blind?) to show me.
I'd seen photos of this place where not one stone,
for blocks, except these, stood on another one.

The Table

As in a Bonnard,
or maybe just
the Bonnard on this postcard,
the woman sitting at the table
seems to be part of the table.
Places are set for two others,
but they seem to be late,
or can't come, or fell down,
or decided it was too
lovely a day to sit
in front of a brown door,
fingering the few cherries
left in the basket, eating
another roll, a second peach.
Besides, the woman is hardly there.
Her face is turned away,
her attention fixed
on something her hands
are doing in a bowl.
Her voice barely rises
above a mumble. Hair
falls down the side of her head
as though it didn't matter
that eighty or so years later
we would be walking
along a coastline in the rain,
having once again, and elsewhere,
found the soul's own
flickering habitation, aghast

at the drenched way
the feathers clung
to the bones of the dead gannet
tossed among
the gannet-colored stones.
The wind whiffled its way
down the coast, looking
for something likely,
a feather, a blade of grass,
a finger, whatever
is made of wind or has
the lift and surge
of its idlest inclinations
knitted to its wrist.
The clouds moved off
mumbling to themselves,
places
already set for us.

Delicate Bait

The shell of the meal broken
and sucked clean, the ocean
chewing up the beach beyond the palms
made it seem that eating a simple meal
there by the ocean at night
on an island heaved up millennia ago
in fiery explosions, and the fish
having leapt out of the same water,
bodies of a movement of that sea,
ocean larger than anything
on earth, would suffice. That we should come
and go, eating the few thousand meals,
a few hundred fish, a room full of grains,
that we should put the world in our mouths
and swallow, become the fish,
the deer, the goat, the field of wheat,
walking graveyard with no stones, body of death
and the world. Out of the fish
and our sitting there, out of our
being together briefly in that place,
our scattered and gathered trying-to-be,
one to the other, less evanescent,
less brief and accidental, something,
so that when, in the impending hour,
oblivious, hour of cancellation and woe,
we turned back to our lives, whatever they were,
we would have, or keep, maybe a phrase,
a sense of the light, the look
of the fish arranged on its bier of rice,

the voice of the ocean, continuous, around us,
the burning of that hour together, something,
something even memory cannot reach,
wave that rolls across an ocean
only to fall gratefully onto the sand.

On the north side of the island,
region of small icons and cairns,
in the voice of that place, tumble
of rock back into the sea from which it came,
people stack one rock on another,
two or three, a cluster,
sometimes a single rock set out alone
on the edge of that other rock,
the island itself, saying here,
a flame in a red dress, I was here, and the fish
is a part of my body, and I thank
the fish and the cook and the person
who brought it to me and those
at the other tables making cairns
out of words and gestures,
glances in every direction.
It was beginning to slide, wash
back into the silence from which it came.
It was happening to me, to us,
and I was watching it, lifted
one fork at a time into my mouth,
into the mouths of the others, those
I was with, those I was almost with,
those gone and going before,
those for whom I am the one going before,
scattering, as when alarmed,

not scattering really, but moving just beyond
the ends of our fingers,
when, swimming among them,
we reach out to touch them,
almost become one ourselves,
fish in the sea.
And, that more delicate bait,
the you and the me.

An Afternoon's Walk

Up and down over the ledges on Pitchoff
yesterday, amazed at the views, burnish of the leaves
in early October, as the world gets ready again
for fall, the beginning of winter, end of another year.

It was only two days ago that my aunt died.
Ninety years old, and she just gave out.
Penny said she spent her last month or two sitting
in a chair with her eyes closed, saying nothing.

She had trouble recognizing people, sometimes
even Penny. She was tired. She just saw no way
forward, except on to that other thing people,
in their oddity, their desperation, foolishness,

holiness, too, I suppose, willingly plunge themselves.
As those men did who flew planes into New York,
screaming the name of Allah, believing in death,
believing that death could be surmounted only

by death. I want to know what they were thinking.
But it seems as though we are not here to know
very much. They sit somewhere, or their ghosts do,
with their eyes closed forever, saying nothing.

If you must know something, says the tableau
of our days, you may have to make it up.
So, be careful. The earth is doing its thing again,
paying no attention to us. We wanted so much

to get down into that indifference, that quiet, wild
concentration, slow flame over the rocks,
and somewhere in the inner brain of each of us,
I think we did, chatting our way across

one exposed ledge to the next, happy to be
inventing a world so similar to the world itself
it became the world, before turning down
through steep gullies to the road below.

Alone in the House

Hills, and beyond them mountains.
The edge of a graspable universe,
with a foreground of laid stone
pathway, a bench, a few twists
of some generic flower. A lake
in the middle distance, clouds
along the upper border, a framed
revery, though that's tulips,
I'm sure, along the bottom.
I could almost walk straight
into this picture, except that
a tanned boy passes the window,
his leafblower screaming
at the real leaves. Once again,
I'm drinking a small draught
of my parents' life, trying,
now that one of them is gone,
to savor the secret of it.
On the table in front of me,
a cropped photograph.
Mother's mother, dead now
twenty years. This is the place
where my mother and father
shaped an ending to their life.
Beside the bed, a stack of books.
Hemingway's *A Moveable Feast,*
the essays of E. B. White,
a penholder with tiny clock
frozen at 7:36.

I open a drawer, and under
a gold thimble, orderly stacks
of cards and envelopes, tidy
reminders of mother's hopes
to answer the call of the world,
or, if suddenly called herself,
to be remembered as one
who kept her things in order,
who, when I saw her last,
couldn't remember the name
of the song in her dream, and so
hunted along the piano
for it, her ancient, spotted
bony hands still able
to wring chords I remember
hearing across the whole length
of the house when I was nine
or ten and couldn't imagine what
a sweet embraceable one
was or why she sang to it
so feelingly and long.

Summers at the Lake

Aromas of the pine and gas pump mix,
the sleek, low inboard rocking in its slip.
Something like permanence in the way days
turned slowly on a spit, and in the evenings,
the old stories passed around, followed by
the rattle of the dominos, clink
of ice cubes, lubricated laughter, jokes
you didn't need to get to know they were
funny somehow. It made the world theirs,
a place you could be in and not worry, he,
who had nothing on his mind, anyway,
other than winning, and the daily tremors
six-year-olds have whose mothers have decided
to take their secret with them to the grave.

Planting Trees

I planted trees last summer, seedling pines,
in a place cleared for hay two hundred years
ago. She calls it a grove already,
and promises to put my ashes there.
I say, OK, but can't imagine death.
Not mine, not yet. Besides, we're here, still here.
The soil is sandy, easy to dig into.
The pines aren't fussy. They put their roots down
anywhere. Almost anywhere. The snow
bends them to the ground, but they spring back straight,
if they don't crack. And even if they do,
they shrug it off, a branch here, a trunk there.
The coolness they make in summer, the wind's
soughing. Imagine! Among those little pines.

II

Digging: Metal and Glass

The jars of cold cream, the cans of oil. I pull
a buggy strut, a child's skate, a toy truck,
up out of rooted duff beneath a pine.
Everywhere a tossed salad of glass
fragments, a brittle rattle of crushed tin.
When I think I could be camped on some cold
high col, or caravanning down the sheer
passes above whatever place that was
I read about when I was ten or so,
I think I'd rather lie here in the dirt
under this tree, digging up a life that was
and wasn't mine. This shovel with no handle.
This spike-toothed harrow missing a tooth or two.
This life, that isn't quite mine anyway.

No Distance

Small scribbled shadow in the grass
beneath the propped-up crabapple.
Cottonwoods crumpling paper
in the breeze. And the shaggy
stupefied wag of the fattened
old necks of Norway spruce.
This cattle of motions
and herded grasses bays
for its milking, the milk
of it floating past
on the unhurried seeds. Air
is not air. Down somewhere
in the thickest grass,
stuff no one knows the name of,
plump dirt of the words,
the beetle finds its meat,
the sparrow knows to look
over its shoulder when it feeds.
There is no distance
to the distance. Water
wants to slide downhill,
and the huge old Galapagoan
snapper on the pathway, eyeballs
marbled blind and leeches
dangling off her tender,
leathery underflesh, raises
her hatcheted head, sniffs
as if remembering,
and keeps on pawing.

For Instance

The pigeon eyes me
from her nest above the stacks
of upturned tables.
With the suddenness
of a leaf
along a branch,
I turn and look.
I have tried walking
and not walking.
I am not walking now.
Anger and tenderness,
those old cronies.
There is anger
in tenderness,
tenderness in
getting the thing
finally
to lie down.
I have tried caring
and, naturally, the opposite.
I am still trying to find
the opposite.
The phone
goes on ringing.
Gray sky and blue, black sky
under the stars, gray rose
tinting the underclouds at dusk.
Out on the lake, a sailboat
fidgets with the wind.

The wind fidgets back.
I have tried a little smoke,
a little love, a little
worrisome, uncertain motion
up and down the highway,
crow flight
over the road,
field filled with water,
field rained on
all day long, field
incapable of more,
half-eaten carcass
of a warbler on the grass,
plain wooden table
in a plain wooden room, water
rising at the bank,
rising and breaking,
rising and turning back,
breaking and turning back.
I have walked along the Wabash,
along the muck along the Wabash,
in spring,
and stood there
considering.
Distance, too.
It's there, part
of the daylight's invention.
What is it
in the waspfloat and tremor,
clouds billowy and rust
above Gary, East Chicago?

I drive into a town,
and no one's there.
Pickups, washer, broken swing.
I look at the houses,
the rain-blackened windows.
Why should there be trees?
Or green? I can't think
why there should be green.
I drive away
relieved. Perplexed, of course,
but relieved.
And here is a bridge
with river underneath.
The river trembles.
The raft,
nine rusty barges
belted together,
swings
slowly outward
into the current.
Men in yellow slickers
walk the glassy edges,
the suddenness of everything,
Kentucky,
of there being boundaries
at all,
cities, towns, people,
of there being
cars, anything,
words on a page.

Now and a Pile of Sticks

I don't get a sense of the difference
between now and a pile of sticks.
Though the one I keep in a stack
by the back door, and the other I burn.

The Way Two Horses Stand

The way two horses stand next to one another in a field,
and we are coming into the village in a car to have lunch
with old friends at the deli, and the sun and the wind
are helping one another slowly up a difficult stairway.

The way the fox crossing the field lowers its head and squints
as though swimming underwater through a stream of bugs,
the kind that only that morning found there was a world
and have only till evening to solve the mysterious silence.

The way the eastern phoebe in the nest above the door holds
fiercely to the hatching of her five white eggs, round as peas,
and though we come and go, wondering whether it matters
if stars collide, guarding its muddy purchase on the possible.

The way the clouds amble along whispering among themselves.
The way, the daily way, we have of deciphering what they're saying.
The way sky darkens before rain, and the rain hesitantly
steps down into the grass, as though into freshly drawn bathwater.

Reasonable Conversation

Reasonable conversation as I cross
the street. I'm having reasonable
conversation, and the street responds
with sand. I'm talking to a dog,
dog in a picture (the dog is barking
in the picture), and the melting snow
agrees. Twigs are everywhere,
even in the trees, holding reasonable
conversation with the air. The point
the morning's working up to
seems practical and clear. It's there.
I can hear it in the jay's flat screech
and see it, too, in the woman
struggling with a bag on her way to
who knows what in bright skinny leggings
(struggling in those leggings),
and no doubt, too, having quick,
amicable chat with some sparrows.
Or the Pope. The mayor's waiting
at the door (me, I can't believe it,
a poet) for my proposal about air.
We need to keep it moving, never still.
The mayor is delirious with agreement.
Nothing must be ever still.
And a good thing, too, since nothing is,
except the obvious. The obvious doesn't
blink. The obvious is obvious

and likes it that way. No need
for conversation with the obvious.
None of your reasonable, even
interchanges. None of your spontaneous
and continuous. Looking into puddles,
noticing the rust-and-rusty-laughter
kind of thing. None of that.
Applause, rather. Silence.
Heavy and obvious.
Several stars run a red light.

These Days

I sit on the stump end of a fallen tree,
scribbling. The sun has the whole sky
to itself. I have the field.

These days I don't need to see it
to know it's there. A great crested flycatcher
purrts somewhere in the trees behind me

as a piece of the rotted oak breaks under my foot.
"Expect nothing," the roshi said
to the man who came to his mountain.

I reach down for a handful
of the cool, dry, compacted stuff.
It crumbles completely in the hand.

Local Habitation

> *If we comprehend a social system as a lifeworld,*
> *then the steering aspect is screened out.*
>
> *—Jurgen Habermas*

We could start with Andis, Russell, 18,
recently released from the Indiana
Home for Boys. We could also start with
Taylor, Gary, 15, who, the newspaper said,
lived with his father in Chicago until
food and patience ran out. We could
also start with a herd of yaks
on the Gobi Desert, 1922. Wherever
we start, we still have to face Lane,
the cabdriver, listed a bit to one side,
the engine still running and the wipers
wiping rain across a glassy sky.
Cut the "rain across a glassy sky,"
cut the "wiping." There he was, dead,
and the world with its rain and the car
with its various mechanical systems were
doing the breathing for him. Meanwhile,
the governor gripped the podium tight
and told the state, all civilizations
had to kill, just to be civilizations.
That was the way you did it. That was the way
hamburger found its way to the table.
That was the way it came to be formed
into patties. "Execution specialists"
have put the chair in Michigan City

in peak condition for Thursday's event.
Resnover will die sitting down, we hope
on the first ripping jolt, not like last time
when it took three great whacks of that
glassy metallic ejaculation
seventeen minutes to assure prison
officials the man the people wanted dead was.
We have to stand here and watch like a crow,
a crow by the side of the road, waiting
to see if the possum will make it across.
The cab driver lived at the Southern Winds.
The residents said he always had something
to say, a smile. His red Honda motorcycle
still sits tilted in front of the unit
he called home. Andis is said to have wept
at the sight of Lane. "Nobody was supposed
to die." Nobody was supposed to sleep
on the street, either, or wake up covered
with flies. They were going to kill Taylor
in school. The governor wishes he were still
raising his hand, answers clapped to the tips
of his fingers. The engine was left running.
So was the weather. On the Gobi,
a herd of yaks. It's 1922.
What is a residential motel, anyway?
Is the life of a policeman worth more
than the rain? Throw the wiper blades in
as an extra. I feel a terrible
feeling. Maybe it's just anger, old stupid
unlocated pointless anger, and I need
some flimsy rack to drape it over

and dry it out. What are we that we can
scrutinize and weep? The mother of two
straps her babies into their safety seats.
But you don't want to hear the rest of it.
It isn't the story you think, anyway.
None of these things is truly a story.
The law thinks we act on our own,
but nobody goes to their doom alone.
On the Gobi, the wind never stops blowing.
Zoom to the corner of Lincoln and Third,
to the woman waiting for something. Her face.
Imagine the soft clack of the pony's hoofs
on the stones of the Gobi as music.

Free Fall

He didn't like it that someone had said
that thing about him years ago—whatever it was.
He didn't like being noticed in that way.
True, he had a proclivity to being vague
or unnoticed or perhaps to just not wanting
at every moment to declare where he stood.
He was always seeing the other side of things,
having already made the near side a logical choice.
It was being seen he didn't like, since the ways
of doing that in the world were never full enough.
Some were fuller than others, though, and stung
with an exactness that drove him farther up
the Himalayas of his hidden nature, insisting,
to himself, of course, that there were steeper peaks,
remoter reaches, of the self where, as the metaphor
leads us to say, it was difficult to breathe.
Where, in fact, you could step right out of yourself,
as out of a plane in flight, and be the whole blue sky,
if you wanted, a pile of cloud rushing to the edge
of the observable universe, or a man dead in a field.

No, it was some other condition he suffered from,
a belief, you might say, that life had to be more
than these few months held together by string,
this succession of hopes and tasks, meetings
and declarations of undying love, books read
on airplanes, airplanes passing over continents
and oceans as the hero stumbled through his paces
toward ends infinitely interpretable, resolutions

in a grassblade, finalities of an eyelash,
while a grunting pig rooted among the rubbish
in the yard or the slow leak in human attention
brought its dirigible to the ground. He was sure
there was a thing here to be seen and understood,
if only he could keep from sealing it off
by a too-hasty acquiescence to the bandages
of the moment. Which left him, oddly enough,
with moments only as bandages and a wound
he kept trying to describe to doctors of increasing
remoteness, doctors of remoteness itself, physicians
of the fall—free, blind, and wingless—through space.

Wire Fences

"Nobody travels a long way to gaze
at wire fences." Nobody we know,
at any rate. Though I've seen one somewhere
recently I thought had the sprung tautness
I like in a line of verse. No slack,
and the only thing between me and a field
I'd otherwise have looked past or beyond,
a single strand of wire surrounding it.
Sometimes, when I'm out alone, following
the line between the neighbor's land and mine,
I find a broken post with a tangle
of rusted wire nailed to it. Neither he
nor I put it there. Those who did have left
this valley. And the lives they lived went with them.

Man Walking Home with a Stick

A limb, really. A piece of tree.
As though it were night. Or day.
As though there was no hurry.

A man on a high wire.
Saying the names of streets.
Or birds. Whispering cloud or sunlight.

A man walking along.
A stranger among us, counting
his steps, knowing the number

of days, things lying about,
keeping track of the crows,
of the kinds of lichen

on the back of a smooth stone.
Holding on to a rail, the ship
beginning to tilt.

Walking along the line of a cloud,
holding a stick in his hand,
watching sky shift.

At the corner of First and Woodlawn
forever, at the sign where no one
stops, stopping.

A house throws off its soffit
like an old life.
A feral arrangement of weeds

and litter gathers at the bumper
of a car too rusted to care.
A man carrying a stick

is no stranger than a feather,
no lighter than a blade of grass,
no wider than sunlight.

Weather plunges
into the universe. A piece of moon
sticks to the handle of a rake.

The fork shoves into the dirt
and sucks as it comes up
bleeding with worms.

The man with the stick
comes to the edge of several things
at once, a moving point

among moving points,
divining a way among people
and cars, among trees

that offer him bits of themselves,
the fire that feeds them,
the silky ash.

Middle of the Street

Cloud drapes over the trees on the far side
of the hedge. Beyond that, a kind of gray
that simulates the way to heaven.
I used to think the dead could watch us. God,
I was sure, knew what I thought. It was only
the living I had any chance to elude.
And look what a shambles I made of that.
Last night in the grocery store. Last week
at the mall. I tried wearing my Just
One of the Guys disguise. I even went
to the movies. I cried. I ate a tub
of popcorn. It's not a matter of wanting,
really. I look across the tops of a few
thousand trees and try not to blink. I say
let's reinvent a few phrases calmly over
some chilled wine on the deck, the sun draining
light out of the sky and the swallows
stuttering over the water in the bay.
And the bay staying there, and the swallows,
and the few fine phrases and the moon spun
purely out of darkness. And the darkness.
I think it was darkness I scrambled up
all those years ago, and though I wanted
to leave it, I never have. Wanted to,
but didn't. A crow out there finally
has my attention. I've got a few things
I want to say, too, but I keep dropping them.
Something will eat everything, even

the crow. Even the unimaginable
flesh by the side of the road. Even you.
Finally, you are here just long enough
to tell us what it was like.
Not what it was like, but what it was,
to walk down the middle of the street
in a fog so dense you couldn't see your feet.
You made your way gingerly across the square,
found the train, boarded it, and got there.

Farmers

To confront, immediately and directly if possible,
the bare bones of existence.

—Edward Abbey

It's not the sort of thing they thought about,
though it's probably what they did.
Find a way to cheat the earth into
a decent crop of hay, wheedle a few
spavined Jerseys out of their milk, and not
take a vacation, ever, from the worry,
the valley, its low hills clustered thick
around some rocks the river hasn't budged
in ten thousand years. Tools and their uses
scattered along the fence, only a few
of which I recognize, but, clear or not,
I carry what I can lift out to the field,
and make a few arrangements out of things
that, if they didn't give life, made it work.

Glancing out the Window

This is what I think. I think this getting up
in the morning and going out the door
is a kind of waiting. The same with this
coming home in the evening, full of news.
I think this glancing out the window
at the neighbor's roses has nothing to do
with the neighbor or his roses. I think
it is all a looking-for, a sitting-still,
a confidence that underneath the eye
or behind the exhaustion of the sun
a semblance lurks.
                                        No, not a semblance. This
would be the thing that semblances would be,
if they could. This would not be other than
it is. And would be here, now. And is.

Accidental Archaeology

Holding a handful of hammered metal
up to the light, heel of an old boot, belt,
belt buckle, harrow, fondling a bent flange.
Bolt next to sprocket next to crushed bucket.
Spade folded in half, plow, pitchfork missing
a single tine, runners of a horse-drawn sleigh.
The field hasn't been farmed for fifty years,
farmhouse burned to the ground, people dispersed,
though I've been told that the old woman
across the road has the same name as the road.
Is that her mother's enameled pan, blue,
shot through with rust, I pulled out of the grass,
a bowlful of thick moss? Who drank this whiskey?
Milk of kindness, as well as magnesia,
tumbles through these rocks on a current
of silica, brittle tin, and twisted wire.
It's a dirt that has almost the same name
as the dirt, a pour similar to ice
when it lets what it has in its grip go,
glitter and thickness, the promise of rot.

Farming

Conversion of the forests. Making hay
where swamps made little more than habitat
for snakes. Snakes turned into devils. And wolves,
whose howling gave the wilderness its name.
The enemies of farming, God. The pastor in
the pastoral, the shepherd in his fold.
For a long time I thought of it as rock,
the given, stuff the heavings of the planet
left there. The way of nature, not its end.
Though we are nature, too, we say, not just
apologists for the harsh husbanding
that feeds us, gives us images of love,
ease, beauty, and a way for God to be
among us. Even the rock, they said, was cleft.

The Place We Came Ashore

The small colony of black noddies
tucked up into its cave. The way
every time we go there, little spurts
of clouddust or shoremist spatter us,
and on each of the narrow ledges up under
the glowering volcanic cap, birdlime streaks
downward in a floral exuberance.
The sea comes heaving in on time, every time,
and the birds flap out now and again just
over the top of it. Try as hard as we can
to prevent it, they disappear into the light
shredding itself to pieces on the sea's back.
I don't know why, when I think of it, I think
this is the place love found us, away
almost from our own nature, looking back
up into the land as though from another world.
As though this was the place we came ashore
all those thousands of years ago, looking
for what we would learn to call each other.

Dispersal

I ripped the blossom open. They were falling
anyway. It was time. I rubbed the small
smear of pollen, finger and thumb, against
a tree. Perhaps a rat, the wind, something,
would take it from there, move it to a piece
of dirt, a wing, whatever drift that is
in steep slants of sunlight that disappears
when we enter it. I was passing by.
It was on the ground. I picked it up.

The Meadow

I hum the meadow, broad and flat,
and a little marshy at one end,
with numerous grasses stuffed,
with bushy matter dotted, snakes,
and a multitude of flowers,
all ringed with cottonwood and elm,
with bug noise, bird song everywhere,
and air, always a little air
moving, or great gales thrashing.
A world in which the weed is free,
and there is no rancor anywhere,
except perhaps among the birds,
who warble when they squabble.
The sun looks down and smiles.
It sees itself reflected there,
a round, bland glow,
a slowness in the scheme of things.
It wants to join us there, and does,
turning the tiny head of the six-
petalled yellow star grass upward
and the tall, thick-stemmed rattlesnake weed.
What are those clumps of broad, long leaves
with the small, gray roll of leaf inside?
I want to know, but have no need
to know today. I run my finger
along the hairy stem instead,
and the female red-winged blackbird flips
out of the grass ten feet away.
I know a nest is near, and though
I'd like to see the little eggs

couched in their cup of woven grass—
just look, and never touch—I say
out loud, OK, I won't go near.
I know the eggs are there, the three-
to-five my bird book says there are,
pale blue and spotted brown and purple.
I walk away, and the meadow breathes
a sigh. Sometimes I wish I weren't
a big galoot who puts his foot
down there where a hundred thousand things
live out their lives in half a day.
And I wish I knew a way to end
this song, since, like a meadow, songs
can lead the singer into sand,
marshy places where the boot
sucks down and the muskrat runs for cover.
So, like a meadow, I'll just go
up to these cottonwoods and stop.

Naming the Grasses

A fly lands on my sleeve, and, right away,
the prairie shifts. A breeze that almost
isn't strums the stalks of last year's grasses.
The shadow on the clusters of Lovegrass
slides slowly down the spikelets as the sun
climbs. India Lovegrass, Little Barley. Names
I take from a book. Two blackbirds and a brown
thrasher. The blackbirds fly a perfect close
formation over the cattails, the one
unable to shake the other free. How
do they decide which one leads? That's love,
I guess, the kind that bends the heads
of these bushy clusters of something toward
the sun. Everything does that. I go back
to my book. Downy Oatgrass, it tells me.
Maybe the yellow warbler to my left
will let me see him. Maybe not. He's got
a nest nearby he's keeping out of sight.
Praise the grasses, thick and nameless, thick
and puzzling to us all. Two deer bound by
and slide in quickly among the high bleached
stubble of last year's prairie. Baby bucks,
their horns velvet. I turn to look at two
blackbirds chasing a crow and see the slight
sag in the field down toward the cattails
where the summer river has almost gone to sleep.
I may not ever know Little Quaking Grass,
but I believe it. Wolftail doesn't grow here,
but I can see how someone might have stopped

in a field somewhere. Oregon, Nebraska.
Of course, it wouldn't have been a field like this,
bounded by houses, power lines, a highway.
There would have been no Nebraska. Few things
he saw would have had names then. There it was,
as the book says, densely tufted, unlike
any grasses he knew. Slender Wheatgrass.
Slimstem Muhly. We live to name things.
Seed of the cottonwood goes by all day,
weighing barely more than the air. One snags
on the stalk of some plant that last year bloomed.
It didn't know it had a name. It bloomed instead.

Yes

Over cereal and coffee, I watch
the suits rush by. How lucky, a cubicle
to go to, stack of heady memos, desk,
lights left on all night, waiting for the breath
this quickmarch brings to slumbering pads
and paperclips. Windows mirror windows,
clouds clamor past, while a slow blue fuselage
floats its airy passengers back to earth.

Two days ago, wandering the city,
we passed a man asleep on the street, pitched
forward over a sheaf of papers, pen
in hand, caught in the middle of a thought
fatigue, to call it that, had robbed him of.

This morning, an executive, full dress,
grey pinstripe suit, slim leather briefcase, slipped
out of a cab just as it pulled up at the curb.
The effortless emergence from the car,
the practiced stride away into the closed
compartments of the city's secret life,
this must be what it is to run the world,
we said, a flash of quick movement, turn
of a head in a milling crowd, and, somewhere
in back of us, the tinkle of broken glass.

I'm at a table now, second coffee
of the day cooling at my wrist, when she
comes by, a line of perspiration down

her cheek, efficient, anxious, rag in hand,
who, two days ago, blushed taking our plates.
"It's my first day," she said. Today is her
third day. Her life is underway now, hers.
I know nothing about her, but she will be
what all of us have been, happy and sad,
and, long life or short, hers will be the kind
someone will stumble on in a stray moment,
one of those rattling eternities
on the tube, and think, this is what I meant
back then when everything had luster but
no depth, someone approached you on the path,
then turned away, only to come back, face
blurred, memory obliterated, hands
held outward as in supplication, prayer,
maybe fear, laughter.
                                        The calm day waves at us,
indifferent to the images snapped off
its dying branches. Another image, yes.
Another grab at the handle, at the rope
thrown out over the water. At the water
itself.
            We will go to the theater
tonight, down by the river. Water plays
the role of river and river the role
of mother and father. Cormorant and gull,
one of them in it, the other above.
Afterwards, the pubs closed, the train packed
elbow to armpit, satchel, baggage, grip,
all of us headed home, maybe the next stop,
out to a place called Epping, end of the line.
A cell phone rings, and suddenly someone,

only a seat away, is saying loudly
to none of us, “Yes, it was lovely. Yes.”
After a pause, “I’ll be there in ten minutes.”
Half of us look at our watches, wonder
what could be so desirable and near,
a mere six hundred seconds from here.

Bad Sit

for Ethan

I've been sitting recently with friends,
hoping to locate the needle of repose
in what is otherwise a pile of thought.
I'm not supposed to notice anything,
really, but the back of my friend's neck
is there, and I notice the hair going
its own several ways across the shank
of it, the muscles tensing as he tries
to swallow his saliva without being
anywhere near it. These things come at me
in a tidal froth, the world saying, you
thought you'd get away from us, didn't you.
So I try looking at the floorboards.
A single floorboard. A small dent in a
single floorboard. But before long I'm swimming
in the history of a piece of wood.
It's an old board. It came out of a tree
a hundred years ago. And that dent.
How did it get there? Did someone fall?
Did someone drop her favorite china
pitcher on the floor? Was it, as I sense,
her last night in this huge draughty structure?
Did she leave these mountains at dawn, a few things
thrown into a bag, a portmanteau, and race
down to the train, hissing on its siding,
back to the city, back to her sister
in Athens who, dying in her arms, told her,

finally, the family secret, which
drove her to a life of crime in Barcelona?
All we have to remember this fearful
tragedy by is a small dent in a board
in a house in the mountains far from the sea,
where the wind blows rain against the glass,
glass so old things swim through it like a spill,
and a few of us try holding the mind still.

Wind from the South

Quick squiggles shaded in with light and dark washes. Little starveling twisted dogs. People with heads as big as their bellies. Make-up and dirt. Punchinellos all over the place, even the swaddling one, the one riding a horse, played with by a centaur, leaping and jiggling. Here's where Tiepolo jotted down, jotted and passed on. Life as a trick dance, scratchings and ecstasies in corners where the stableboy slept in his own piss, where people called on their deaf gods and their deafer neighbors. Angels everywhere, even the Almighty up in the air, spurted at by cloud and winged adorati. In the thick air of an early cathedral, Ambrose receiving Augustine. Slashes of light blazing them up like coals. Which of them speaks? The drawing is too quick to say. Both astonished to feel the tug of eventual sainthood. Gaze falling back through centuries of holy graffiti, plus the burl of this morning in January, Indiana, southern Indiana, late twentieth century, cloud cover steady, wind from the south.

The Fox

Starts at its own alertness.
Does not sleep completely
or for long. Sleeps on the run.
Always has two errands:
to get where it's going
and to miss nothing. Knows
it is prey, yet loves
the getting away. Has a long,
bushy, significant tail,
which it holds out like
a reason for being. Jumps
at a whimper somewhere
under the snow, swerves
at a single filament
of the complicated air,
suggestion of muskrat,
scratch of falling star.
Harkens at the beetle,
is stopped by the oddness
of dropped limb, hissing
of grasses, succulent grub.
Came once, when called, halfway
across the field. Almost
forgot what we were, where.
The two of us, standing there.

Free Coaster

The coaster that came with my eight-dollar purchase of gas
is, of course, an advertisement. Santa surprised getting a Coke
out of the refrigerator by little Willie in his pajamas.
The door stands open, and a soft milk-white glow pours
onto the cheek of Mr. Claus, the back of his left hand
(the one holding the bottle), and, of course, over the deep
pile of his fire-engine-red Santa suit. Light spills, too,
onto the floor. You can see towheaded Willie is delighted,
though he stands in an oddly reflective posture, bent
at the waist, with his hands behind his back. His sleeper
is pink. Indeed, except for the blues and blue-grays
of the refrigerator (and the whiteness of the light), everything
is touched by red. The shadows at the back of Willie's head,
Santa's brown boots, the Coke, everything, as though red
were the color of appetite and happiness and surprise.

Someone painted this image. It is made to make us think
of the past. The bottle opener in Santa's hand, the bottle
itself, the rosy-cheeked innocence, not just of the boy,
but of the old man, too. Though it doesn't invoke that
by-now wearying hope for a horse-drawn innocence
and snows as deep as silence can make them, this image
would nevertheless want us to turn back toward something,
a moment, say, when a guileless faith in unearthly events
mixed easily with the machine, with commerce itself.
There stands the refrigerator, with its door flung wide
and its shelves heaped with abundance, and the light
of that abundance shines down onto the hand and the beard
and finally the floor, as though all light fell, even

when it touched the innocent thievery of the family's
store of Coke. What Santa wouldn't want a Coke on a night
like this? And the little boy finding he hadn't been lied to.

I look in the wrinkled cloth for the artist's initials,
some secret code in the hairs of Santa's beard. But
the only artists acknowledged are the people who make
Coke. The bottle is turned our way so we can see the
familiar script. And on the back, the people of Taiwan,
or some of them, who made the coaster itself. Stamped
out by the millions, like art in an age of mechanical
reproduction, the coaster is a marvel of engineering,
with its cork base and its glassy four-color print
separated by a layer of gray paper. Like the piece
to a puzzle. Like a puzzle already put together.
Or one that was never taken apart. What must the people
of Taiwan think of the fat little man in red? How
did he get in the house? Why is the boy unafraid?

Crystal of Gloom

The plane hidden in the cloud roaring low over
the gray rain ripped out of the sky and the rocks
slick with it and the loaded flowing voluminous
sagging of the soaked branches of the Norway spruce
and the grass going back to the greenness that fled
from the spring as the drought of summer stole and
steadily parched the land and the seed pods cracked
and began cracking and the brown that is truly green
stripped, its newness the newness of lettuce, gone
or going down the slanted bank of summer, but here
stripped for a time as the day of unceasing rain
rains down in tatters and takes down with it air
and the movement of air as the cloud comes down
to see what all the fuss of earth is and is about.

And so to the rain we say, you are the rain and are
the real rain that arrives hard and comes down now
and will, that spills into our lives a kind of food
of gloom, clear mothering milk and crystal of gloom,
and asks only that at some pause in the flood and flow,
we stand out in it, if only to show that we can,
to say this is a world we have no way to avoid,
should we want to, no way to keep from falling,
the rain of everything from potatoes to black silk,
from silk to the small worm, rain of rot that comes down green,
rain that, because it falls, must have a height
from which to pitch, an up to which it goes when down
is done, when the cloud decides to move or the wind
says rain there's a world, and the world says yes I rain.

Gully

A cool dry spring breaks into thunder and all-day rains.
Grasses darken.
Clusters of wild geranium purple the damp
shadows under two shagbark hickories.
A solitary sandpiper lifts its wingtips
to see what mud
imagination's mirror has in mind.

I stood last night by the creek, calling an owl down
from the ridge top.
It called back, but it would not move. On the far side
of the ridge, the faint wail of a peewee.
It has come back from somewhere carrying a song.
The muskrat drags
the sodden banks for its litter again.

Mud and sticks. A field mouse in the grass. Gnats. Little nubs
of growth thrust out
at the tips or joints of reddish twig ends. Nothing
goes by without coming into the mind
of something as food. Crows pecking through gravel. Slugs.
Sandpipers
scittering up wet sand. Raccoons in trash.

My guess is these tangled bushes keep brooding at bay
in me. Though some
rank misanthropy seems to drive me toward this raw
poetry of things that do not know us,
or if they do, skulk in darkness like black mosses

stuck to the backs
of seeping caves. Like birds I'll never see.

Some days I'd rather live in a gully the wind calls
heaven, than here
among the dishes and the dust. I've had enough
milk to keep a hundred cows in harness,
more opinions than ten thousand politicians
could squeeze into
a twenty-pound sausage of our laws. Still,

the ants keep marching over the threshold, looking for
some small sliver
of something left out on the counter too long, or
that vague odor of abraded skin rubbed
off on the chair back last night as I felt my way
once more across
the room in the dark on the way to bed.

Love Song, in Phoebe

Little cloudlets frozen in their leap across the sky,
wind shushing in the trees.
The bluejays shriek, and the chickadees, agreeing,
stick an extra note in their song.
No one ever told me how sugary
the milkweed blossom smells.
I got to find out for myself.
It was only yesterday I saw my first Wood Nymph
and knew it. Dark bitter chocolate,
its flight the shape of wandering avidity.
I hear a goldfinch go by,
and, looking up, I tell myself I see it.
Why not? Who can it hurt?
The bluebird hawks above the new-cut grass.
Maybe I should take the side of the beetle this time,
but the bluebird won't let me.
The pair of bluebirds. Do they feel
this undershove, this balloon of giddiness? Do they
walk up and down the road for sixty years,
believing in bliss, bliss that is only an inch away?
I think I may have got across that inch, at last,
about fifteen minutes ago.
I was looking at the maple tree
and listening to a cow bawling in the distance.
I thought, two bluebirds, together,
in the same tree for three seconds.
Nothing happened exactly,
but I could feel my mind slipping,

slipping out of its old harness.
It's a beautiful harness, really. It has such thick,
leathery, mule-bedraggled straps.
But I took it off anyway, or maybe it just slipped off
when I wasn't looking,
and I sat there sipping wind out of a bush
and hearing the first phoebe in weeks
say, meadow my meadow.
In Phoebe, of course.

Note

The quote at the beginning of "Wire Fences" comes from *Dry Stone Walls* by Lawrence Garner.

Acknowledgments

The author would like to thank the editors of the following journals where the poems indicated, or early versions of them, were first published:
Arts Indiana: "At the Mall, Late," "Why We're Here";
Big Muddy: "Naming the Grasses," "Repairman";
Breeze: "Local Habitation";
The Cortland Review: "Love Song, in Phoebe," "The Way Two Horses Stand";
Crazyhorse: "Delicate Bait," "Museum of Local History";
Denver Quarterly: "Free Fall," "The Place We Came Ashore";
The Eleventh Muse: "Thrown Back Light";
The Evansville Review: "Reading the Latest History of the Bomb," "Repairman";
Farmers' Market: "Venice, 1979";
Green Mountains Review: "No Distance";
Hayden's Ferry Review: "Retirements in the Neighborhood";
Kentucky Poetry Review: "Glancing out the Window";
Laurel Review: "Free Coaster," "Reasonable Conversation";
The MacGuffin: "The Table";
North American Review: "Motels";
North Dakota Quarterly: "There We Are";
Oberon: "Outside of Town";
The Ohio Review: "Crystal of Gloom," "Gully";
Ploughshares: "Listening";
Poetry: "The Fox";
Poetry East: "Go Ahead";
Poetry Northwest: "For Instance," "Truth of the Matter";
PoetsUSA.com: "An Afternoon's Walk";
Rhino: "Man Walking Home with a Stick";
River City Review: "To Molly on Her Sixteenth Birthday";
Spoon River Poetry Review: "Aunt El," "Bad Sit," "Farmers," "Now and a Pile of Sticks";
Sycamore Review: "Strange Bloom";
Talking River Review: "Clearing in the West";
Tar River Poetry: "Alone in the House," "Destin," "For a Christening in Innishannon," "These Days";
Threepenny Review, "The Meadow."

Thanks to the Chester H. Jones Foundation for giving a prize to "Why We're Here" and to *The MacGuffin* for giving one to "The Table." Many of these poems were started, polished, or completed during several residencies at the Ragdale art colony in northern Illinois. My continuing gratitude goes to the board and staff of that organization. "Wind From the South" first appeared in *A Linen Weave of Bloomington Poets*, ed. Jenny Kander (Lexington, Ky.: Wind, 2002).

About the Author

Roger Mitchell is the author of seven previous works of poetry and a work of nonfiction, *Clear Pond: The Reconstruction of a Life*. His work has received several awards, including the Midland Award in Poetry, The John Ben Snow Award, a Lilly Open Fellowship, the 2001 River Styx International Poetry Award, prizes from the Chester H. Jones Foundation and The MacGuffin, plus two fellowships each from the Indiana Arts Commission and the National Endowment for the Arts. His work has appeared in more than thirty anthologies. He taught for many years in the English department at Indiana University-Bloomington, where he taught both literature and creative writing. Now retired, he divides his time between Bloomington and Jay, New York. In spring 2002, he was an Artist-in-Residence in the Everglades National Park.

About the Book

Delicate Bait was designed and typeset by Amy Petersen, with help from Amy Housely. The typeface, Monotype Dante, was designed by Giovanni Mardersteig. The cover was designed and typeset by Jodi Gabor.

Delicate Bait was printed on 60-pound Dexter Offset Natural and bound by Thomson-Shore of Dexter, Michigan.